Inside the NFL

THE
SAN FRANCISCO
49ERS

BOB ITALIA
ABDO & Daughters

Published by Abdo & Daughters, 4940 Viking Drive, Suite 622, Edina, Minnesota 55435.

Copyright © 1996 by Abdo Consulting Group, Inc., Pentagon Tower, P.O. Box 36036, Minneapolis, Minnesota 55435 USA. International copyrights reserved in all countries. No part of this book may be reproduced in any form without written permission from the publisher.

Printed in the United States.

Cover Photo credits: Wide World Photos/Allsport
Interior Photo credits: Wide World Photos

Edited by Kal Gronvall

Library of Congress Cataloging-in-Publication

Italia, Bob, 1955—
        The San Francisco 49ers / Bob Italia
        p.   cm. -- (Inside the NFL)
Includes index.
Summary: A brief history of the players, coaches, and games of one of the best teams in the National Football League.
        ISBN 1-56239-466-5
        1. San Francisco 49ers (football team)--juvenile literature. 2. National Football
        League--juvenile literature. [1. San Francisco 49ers (football team)--History. 2.
        Football--History.] I. Title. II. Series: Italia, Bob, 1955— Inside the NFL.
GV956.S3I83   1995
796.332'64'0979461--dc20   95-16472
                                                                      CIP
                                                                      AC

CONTENTS

Simply the Best

When football dynasties come to mind, no team has more claims to greatness than the San Francisco 49ers. Their five Super Bowl wins are tops in the National Football League (NFL). And they have racked up more winning seasons and divisional titles than any other franchise.

San Francisco 49ers fullback Frankie Albert follows a block against the Browns in 1951.

Some of the NFL's greatest players have worn 49ers uniforms. One player—Joe Montana—may be the greatest quarterback to ever play the game. All Montana did was win four Super Bowls in four tries—all during the 1980s.

His successor, Steve Young, has already won a Super Bowl title and has the talent to be as great as his predecessor. But unless Young can match Montana's accomplishments, the ghost of Joe Montana will always haunt him. Even so, Young has already set passing records that Montana never achieved.

**Opposite page:
49ers wide receiver Jerry Rice reaches for a pass during the 1990 NFC championship.**

The AAFC

Hugh McElhenny, running back for the 49ers, 1955.

In 1946, the new All-America Football Conference (AAFC) added a team in San Francisco. Two brothers, Tony and Vic Morabito, formed the team. They wanted their hometown to have a professional sports franchise. They called the club the San Francisco 49ers, named for the prospectors who settled around San Francisco during the 1849 California gold rush.

The 49ers did well in their first three seasons. But the AAFC had financial problems. In 1949, the league folded. However, the National Football League (NFL) took four AAFC franchises and added them to their league. One of those teams was the 49ers.

The Morabitos hired a new head coach for the 1950 NFL season. His name was Lawrence "Buck" Shaw. Shaw recruited many NFL castoffs and molded them into a winning team.

One of Shaw's first choices was five-foot eight-inch quarterback Frankie Albert. After playing with the 49ers, he coached the team from 1956 to 1958.

Albert's backup was Yelberton Abraham (Y.A.) Tittle. Tittle had played for the AAFC Baltimore Colts and was looking for a new team. Shaw signed him in 1950.

Tittle became famous for his "Alley Oop" pass near the goalposts. A frequent target was former basketball player R. C. Owens. Owens would time Tittle's throw and jump high to catch the ball.

In 1952, Shaw also added Hugh McElhenny to the team. He became known as "The King" after his first game in a 49ers uniform.

McElhenny refused to carry the ball unless he had a play designed just for him. Albert created the play, and McElhenny ran it for 60 yards on the game's first play. "He's the king," Albert told Shaw. "McElhenny is the king of runners."

Joe "The Jet" Perry also played for the 49ers. In 1953 and 1954, he rushed for over 1,000 yards and scored 50 rushing touchdowns.

Having a talented team, the 49ers got off to a successful start. They had a losing record their first NFL season, but then strung together six straight winning seasons from 1951 to 1956.

The 1957 season ended on a sad note. In a game against the Chicago Bears, the 49ers entered their dressing room at halftime, trailing 17-7. There, Tony Morabito died of a heart attack. Stunned by their owner's death, the 49ers returned to the field and won 21-17.

Hugh McElhenny running against the Rams in 1955.

Brodie and Nolan

Between 1959 and 1967, the 49ers did not have much success. They often finished no higher than third or fourth place in the NFL Western Division. Coaches Red Hickey (1959-1963) and Jack Christensen (1963-1967) had some talented players. But they could not win a championship.

One of those players was quarterback John Brodie, who San Francisco drafted in 1957 from Stanford University. Brodie signed with San Francisco even though other teams offered him more money.

Throughout his career, Brodie survived challenges from other quarterbacks who wanted his job. In 1961, first-round draft pick Billy Kilmer challenged Brodie for the top position. But he did not play as well as Brodie. In 1967, Florida's Steve Spurrier came to the 49ers after winning the Heisman Trophy. But he too could not wrestle the starting quarterback job from Brodie.

Brodie played with the 49ers until 1973. By then, he had led the league in yards, passes, and touchdowns, and won the MVP award in 1970.

Despite Brodie's consistent play, the 49ers could not win a championship. The team needed a winning attitude. To fix the problem, the 49ers hired Dick Nolan as their head coach in 1967.

Nolan knew what it took to be a champion. In the 1950s, he played defensive back for the New York Giants, who won a number of NFL championships. When he retired in 1961, Tom Landry of the Dallas Cowboys hired him as an assistant coach. Nolan remained with the Cowboys until 1967. Then he took the head coaching position of the 49ers.

Under Nolan, the 49ers eventually won divisional championships as San Francisco became one of the highest scoring teams in the

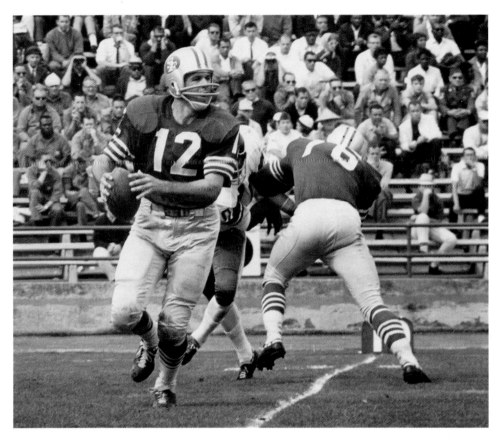

John Brodie, 49ers quarterback, looks for a receiver.

league. Besides Brodie, the 49ers had wide receiver Gene Washington, tight end Ted Kwalick, and running back Ken Willard.

But Nolan knew that defense won championships. Defensive end Cedrick Hardman, linebacker Dave Wilcox, and defensive backs Bruce Taylor and Jimmy Johnson were the standouts. A first-round pick from UCLA in 1961, Johnson played for the 49ers until 1976. He had 47 career interceptions and 615 return yards. Johnson was also named to the Pro Bowl four times. Despite their talent, the San Francisco 49ers were an up-and-down team during Nolan's era. He finally resigned in 1975.

The 49ers hit rockbottom in 1976. In 1977, the Morabitos sold the team to Edward DeBartolo. DeBartolo was the young son of a

Youngstown, Ohio, family who had made their fortune building shopping malls. DeBartolo promised to rebuild the 49ers into a winning team. But in 1978 and 1979, the 49ers had two consecutive 2-14 seasons. Big changes were needed—starting with the head coach. DeBartolo found a gem in Bill Walsh.

49ers wide receiver Gene Washington pulls in a pass from Jim Plunkett.

The Walsh Era

Bill Walsh never played professional football. He was an assistant coach at Oakland in 1966, and with the Cincinnati Bengals from 1967 to 1975. When Bengals' head coach Paul Brown retired in 1975, Walsh expected to get his job. But he was passed up. Even more frustrating, Brown made sure that Walsh could not find a head coaching job anywhere in the NFL.

In 1976, Walsh was an assistant coach with the San Diego Chargers. Then he took the head coaching position at the University of Stanford in 1977 and 1978. There, he won two bowl games in a row. In 1979, DeBartolo called Walsh and offered him the 49ers head coaching job. Walsh immediately accepted.

Walsh spent his first year rebuilding the team. He wanted players who would fit in well with his new system that featured the passing game. While he searched for key players, the 49ers lost their first seven games. The defense was inexperienced and gave up too many points. The only bright spot was quarterback Steve DeBerg, who set new NFL records for pass attempts and completions in one season. Despite DeBerg's efforts, the 49ers won only two games.

However, Walsh proved to be an excellent judge of talent, and his efforts began to pay dividends. Tight end Dwight Clark, defensive backs Ronnie Lott and Eric Wright, and linebacker Keena Turner were drafted. Walsh traded for linebacker Jack Reynolds and lineman Fred Dean. And then there was Joe Montana.

Joe Montana

Joe Montana was born in Monongahela, Pennsylvania. The area produced other great quarterbacks such as George Blanda, Johnny Unitas, and Joe Namath.

When he was young, Montana loved to play sports—especially football and baseball. He became such a good baseball player that the University of North Carolina offered him a scholarship. But Montana wanted to play football.

Montana attended the University of Notre Dame. In his freshman year, he was the seventh-string quarterback, and played sparingly. As a sophomore, Montana came off the bench in an important game against North Carolina. With only 62 seconds remaining, Montana completed four passes for 129 yards and two touchdowns. More importantly, Notre Dame won the contest.

The North Carolina game was the first of many comebacks Montana engineered at Notre Dame. In his final college game at the 1979 Cotton Bowl, the University of Houston led 34-13 in the third quarter. But Montana led his team to a 35-34 victory—the winning touchdown coming in the last two seconds of the game.

When Montana's college career ended, he hoped to be a top draft choice. But many coaches thought Montana was too small to play professional football. San Francisco finally selected him in the third round.

In 1980, the 49ers won their first three games. Steve DeBerg was the starting quarterback. But by the end of the year, Montana had won the job with his heads-up play and scrambling ability. He often teamed up with Dwight Clark on pass plays. The 49ers finished with a 6-10 record, but they were getting better.

The next year, Montana and the 49ers surprised everyone by winning the divisional title. After two of their first three games, the 49ers won 12 of 13 and went to the playoffs for the first time since 1972.

In the playoffs, the 49ers beat the New York Giants 38-24. Now they would have to face the Dallas Cowboys in the NFC title game to earn a trip to the Super Bowl.

Notre Dame quarterback Joe Montana with coach Dan Devine in the Cotton Bowl, 1979.

The Catch

In the NFC title game, the Cowboys took a 17-14 halftime lead. But the 49ers came back in the third quarter with a touchdown to jump ahead 21-17.

In the fourth quarter, the Cowboys kicked a field goal, then scored a touchdown for a 27-21 lead. With just five minutes remaining in the game, the 49ers began a long drive from their own 10-yard line. Montana moved his team down the field with pinpoint passes and timely scrambles. He drove the 49ers all the way to the six-yard line.

On third down, Montana rolled to his right to avoid the Dallas pass rush. Montana saw Dwight Clark cutting across the back of the endzone. He lofted a pass in Clark's direction. Clark leaped high in the air and came down with the ball for the score. "The Catch," as it was known, propelled the 49ers to a 28-27 win and their first Super Bowl berth.

In Super Bowl XVI, the 49ers jumped out to a 20-0 halftime lead over the Cincinnati Bengals. But the Bengals defense stiffened and stopped the 49ers cold while the Bengals' offense scored the next two touchdowns.

In the fourth quarter, the 49ers' Ray Wersching kicked two field goals. A late Bengal touchdown made the score 26-21. But the 49ers defense did not allow another point. San Francisco was finally Super Bowl champions.

In 1982, a players strike ruined the 49ers chances for another Super Bowl title. They did not play well, and finished with a 3-6-0 record. The following season, the 49ers regrouped and stormed back into the playoffs. Montana and Clark were at top form, and rookie running back Roger Craig added to the 49ers offensive attack. On defense, Fred Dean and Ronnie Lott were the stars.

The 49ers faced the Detroit Lions in the playoffs. San Francisco took a 14-9 halftime lead. A third-quarter field goal made it 17-9. But the Lions scored two fourth-quarter touchdowns to grab a late 23-17 advantage. It was time for more Montana magic. Montana led the 49ers on a long, game-winning drive. It ended with a 14-yard touchdown strike to Freddie Solomon.

In the NFC championship game against Washington, the Redskins jumped out to a 21-0 lead after three quarters. But then Washington got the scare of their lives.

The 49ers scored their first touchdown early in the final period, then quickly cut the lead to 21-14 on a 76-yard touchdown pass from Montana to Solomon. With seven minutes remaining, the 49ers tied the score on a touchdown catch by Mike Wilson. But the Redskins kicked a 25-yard field goal with 40 seconds left. This time, Montana could not rally his team.

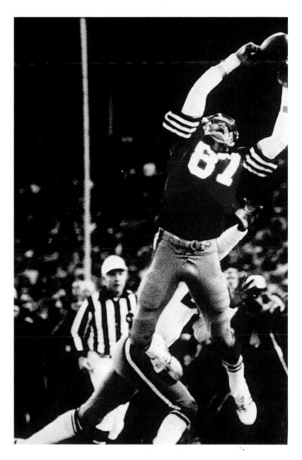

Wide receiver Dwight Clark leaps high to bring down a Joe Montana pass that helped send them to the Super Bowl.

Nearly Perfect

The 49ers bounced back from their disappointing playoff loss to the Redskins by recording the NFL's best record (15-1)—their only loss suffered at the hands of the Steelers at Pittsburgh. Montana had his usual solid season. Wendell Tyler ran for more than 1,200 yards. Defensively, Randy Cross, Keith Fahnhorst, and Fred Quillan made the Pro Bowl. The 49ers entered the playoffs with a nine-game winning streak.

San Francisco easily beat the New York Giants 21-10 in the first round. In the NFC championship game, they faced a tough but inexperienced Chicago Bears team and their number-one-rated defense.

But it was the 49ers defense that shined. They completely shut down the Bears offense while grabbing a 6-0 lead. In the third quarter, Wendell Tyler broke through the endzone on a nine-yard run. A 10-yard pass from Montana to Solomon sealed the win in the fourth quarter as the 49ers won 23-0.

Super Bowl XIX against the Miami Dolphins and Dan Marino looked like a tough matchup. The Dolphins jumped out to a 10-7 first-quarter lead. But then Montana took over in the second quarter. He hit Craig on an eight-yard touchdown pass. Then Montana scored on a six-yard run. A Roger Craig two-yard touchdown run gave the 49ers a 28-16 halftime lead.

The third quarter belonged to the 49ers. Wersching tacked on a 27-yard field goal. Then Montana found Craig on a 16-yard scoring strike. The defense took over in the fourth quarter, shutting down the Miami passing attack. The 49ers had their second Super Bowl win—a 38-16 victory.

For the game, Montana had 331 yards with 3 touchdowns and 59 yards rushing. His efforts earned him MVP honors. Fullback Roger Craig set a Super Bowl record with three touchdowns. And the 49ers defense held Miami to 25 yards rushing with four sacks.

**49ers running back Roger Craig
looks for a hole against Seattle.**

San Francisco 49ers

Hugh McElhenny, running back for the 49ers, 1955.

49ers wide receiver Gene Washington joins the team in 1969.

San Fr
49

John Brodie, 49ers quarterback, is drafted in 1957.

10   20   30   40

4   20   10

Quarterback Joe Montana signs with the 49ers in 1980.

ncisco
ers

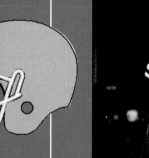

Wide receiver Dwight Clark makes "The Catch" in 1982.

Quarterback Steve Young guides the 49ers to a Super Bowl victory in 1995.

40   30   20   10

Repeat?

San Francisco hoped to repeat their Super Bowl effort in 1985. But the defense slumped badly and Montana got off to a slow start. After seven games, the 49ers were below the .500 mark.

They won five of their next six games to earn a playoff berth with a 10-6 record. But they finished second in the division to the Los Angeles Rams. Montana came back to lead the NFC in passing, and rookie Jerry Rice added more excitement to the passing attack.

But Roger Craig had the best year. He rushed for 1,050 yards and caught a league-leading 92 passes for another 1,106 yards. He became the first player ever to gain a thousand yards in receiving and rushing.

But in the playoffs, the 49ers were bounced 17-3 by the New York Giants.

Montana aggravated a back injury in the 1986 opener and underwent surgery. Many thought his career was over. But Montana returned after the 49ers went 5-3-1.

It was a miracle comeback. Montana sparked the 49ers to the top of the division with wins in the final three weeks over playoff teams. Safety Ronnie Lott led the defense, topping the NFL with 10 interceptions. The 49ers finished with a 10-5-1 record. But once again, the Giants bounced them from the playoffs—this time with an embarrassing 49-3 loss.

In 1987, the 49ers had the best regular-season record in the league (13-2). Jerry Rice set an NFL record with 22 touchdown catches and was voted Player of the Year. Montana won the league passing title and had one of his best seasons. But backup quarterback Steve Young also played brilliantly in his few opportunities, sparking a quarterback controversy. The 49ers led the league in total offense.

Not to be outdone, the 49ers defense was also the NFL's best. Nose tackle Michael Carter and Ronnie Lott were the standouts. The 49ers seemed unbeatable.

49ers quarterback Joe Montana reacts after throwing a touchdown pass to Jerry Rice.

But in the playoffs, the 49ers were surprised at home by the Minnesota Vikings, who jumped out to a 20-3 halftime lead and never looked back. During the game, Montana was injured. Steve Young tried to engineer a comeback, but the lead was just too much. The 49ers fell 36-24, stirring the quarterback controversy. Was Montana's career coming to an end?

In 1988, Walsh declared the competition open for the No. 1 quarterback spot. Montana won the battle, but then was injured, giving Young the opportunity he needed. Roger Craig had his best season. Jerry Rice injured his ankle, which slowed him down the entire season.

**49ers receiver Jerry Rice runs past a
New Orleans defender for a touchdown.**

The 49ers were 6-5 with five games to go. Then everything came together. Led by Montana, San Francisco won four straight to clinch the division title with a 10-6 record. But would they fold again in the playoffs?

In the first round, San Francisco gained revenge over the Vikings with an easy 34-9 win. Montana and Rice hooked up for two scores and Craig added two touchdown runs—one for 80 yards that ended the scoring.

In the championship game against Chicago, Montana picked apart the Bears' NFL-best defense. He completed 17 of 27 passes in 17-degree weather. A 14-3 halftime lead quickly turned into a 21-3 third-quarter advantage. A four-yard Tom Rathman touchdown run ended the scoring and sealed a 28-3 win.

In Super Bowl XXIII, the 49ers battled the Cincinnati Bengals to a 3-3 halftime tie. A third quarter touchdown gave the Bengals a 13-6 lead. But a Montana to Rice touchdown tied the score in the fourth quarter.

With 3:20 remaining in the game, the Bengals kicked a 40-yard field goal to move ahead 16-13. It was time for the drive of the game. Montana started from his own eight with short passes. With 1:15 on the clock, Montana threw over the middle to Rice, who was hauled down at the Bengals' 18-yard line. A quick pass over the middle to Craig gained eight yards. Then Montana hit John Taylor in the endzone for the game-winning score, completing an 11-play, 92-yard drive. Cincinnati was unable to do anything in the 34 seconds they had left. The 49ers had their third Super Bowl victory of the 1980s.

Walsh Resigns

In 1989, Walsh quit as head coach and moved into the broadcast booth. Defensive coordinator George Seifert took his place, and the 49ers kept on rolling.

Montana had his best season ever. He set a new NFL mark with a 112.4 passing rating. Rice broke the team record for touchdown catches in only his fifth season. Craig rushed for over 1,000 yards, and the defense played admirably despite losing free safety Jeff Fuller to a career-ending injury. With a 14-2 record, the 49ers were the best in the NFL.

San Francisco quickly dispatched the Minnesota Vikings 41-13 in the first round of the playoffs. In the NFC championship game, the 49ers rolled over the Rams. Montana passed for 262 yards and two

Head coach Bill Walsh and Joe Montana after defeating the Vikings, 1989.

touchdowns, completing 26-of-30 passes. The 49ers seized a 21-3 halftime lead and coasted to a 30-3 win. Now they had a chance to repeat as Super Bow champions.

It was the best Super Bowl ever—for the 49ers. Montana and San Francisco made football history with their fourth championship of the decade. They also became the first back-to-back winner since the Steelers of the 1970s. Their 55-10 victory over the Denver Broncos represented the biggest margin in Super Bowl history and the most points scored by a Super Bowl team.

Rice caught seven passes for 148 yards and three touchdowns. Montana was 22 of 29 for 297 yards and five touchdowns. At one point, he completed 13 consecutive passes. His efforts earned him his third Super Bowl MVP award.

The 1990 San Francisco 49ers set their sights on NFL history. They wanted to be the first team to win three straight Super Bowls. After finishing the regular season with a 14-2 record, they seemed to be ready to claim their prize.

But age began to catch up with them. Lott missed five games with an injury. Injuries also ruined Craig's season as the running attack disappeared. Only the Montana-to-Rice combination shined.

In the second round of the playoffs, the 49ers easily defeated the Redskins 28-10. But the New York Giants surprised the 49ers in the NFC championship game by stealing a 15-13 win.

Less than five minutes into the third quarter, a 61-yard pass from Montana to Taylor gave the 49ers a 13-6 lead. But with 9:42 remaining, Montana was sacked and knocked from the game with a broken finger. Two New York field goals brought the Giants to within 13-12. Steve Young tried to run out the clock, but Craig fumbled with 2:36 left. The Giants drove for the game-winning field goal and won 15-13.

In 1991, for the first time in more than a decade, the 49ers went an entire season without Joe Montana as he went out with elbow surgery. Even worse, Ronnie Lott and Roger Craig were traded, leaving gaps in the offense and defense.

Steve Young won the NFL passing title and rushed for 415 yards. But he was only 5-5 as a starter and was eventually knocked out of the lineup with a sprained knee. The 49ers finished third with a 10-6 record and did not make the playoffs.

In 1992, Montana played only 30 minutes of the last game of the season. Steve Young had finally become the No. 1 quarterback. He led the NFL in passing with 25 touchdowns and only seven interceptions while rushing for 537 yards and four scores. Ricky Watters emerged as the new running star with 1,013 yards. The 49ers won their division with a 14-2 record, but lost to the revitalized Cowboys 30-20 in the NFC championship game.

49ers quarterback Steve Young looks for a receiver downfield.

Young Takes Over

In 1993, Joe Montana left the 49ers for the Kansas City Chiefs. That left Steve Young to run wild over his opponents. He became the first player in NFL history to lead the league in passing three straight years. Watters rushed for 950 yards and scored 11 touchdowns. Jerry Rice caught 98 passes for 1,503 yards and 15 touchdowns.

The 49ers set a club record with 6,435 yards on offense and scored 473 points—29.6 per game—just two points shy of the team record. San Francisco shook off a 3-3 start to win its 10th divisional title in 13 years and extended a league record of 11 seasons with 10 or more victories. But the 49ers lost the NFC title for the third time in four years—once again to the Dallas Cowboys.

Despite his impressive statistics, everyone wondered if Steve Young could win the big game like Joe Montana did in his years with the 49ers. In 1994, the pressure was on Young to win a record fifth Super Bowl title for San Francisco.

Young responded to the pressure by guiding the 49ers to a 44-14 win on opening day against the Raiders. But in a Week 2 rematch against Montana and the Chiefs, Young came up short, 24-17. San Francisco then won two in a row before being embarrassed 40-8 by the Philadelphia Eagles in Week 5.

That was the turning point for Young and the 49ers. They reeled off five straight wins—including a 21-14 victory over the defending champion Dallas Cowboys.

The 49ers won another five in a row to bring the streak to 10 before dropping a Week 17 game to the Vikings. The game was meaningless, since the 49ers had already clinched home field advantage throughout the playoffs. Rather than risking injury to their top players, the 49ers rested their starting lineup.

The rest seemed to work as the 49ers stayed hot. Against Chicago, the 49ers rolled to a 30-3 halftime lead and routed the Bears 44-15. In the NFC championship game, the team of the 1980s earned a trip to the Super Bowl in 1995.

In the first quarter of the long-awaited showdown with Dallas, the 49ers streaked to a 21-0 lead halfway through the first period. The 49ers then answered every challenge by the Cowboys to put away the champs 38-28. Steve Young was one win away from his first championship.

The game was anticlimactic. In Super Bowl XXIX, the 49ers scored touchdowns on their first three possessions and led 28-10 at halftime. By the end of the third quarter, it was 42-18. The 49ers and Chargers traded scores in the fourth quarter for a 49-26 San Francisco win.

In the game ,Young threw a Super-Bowl record six touchdowns and became the second player in as many years to follow an MVP regular season by winning the same award in the Super Bowl. Young was also the game's leading rusher with 49 yards on five carries.

The victory gave the 49ers their fifth title—more than any other team in NFL history. "I hope we can all separate ourselves from the past," Young said after the game. "I think what we did this year should stand alone."

§

It is the San Francisco 49ers who stand alone in NFL history. No other team has earned more championships. No other team has more of a right to call itself a football dynasty. With players like Young and Rice still in their prime, the 49ers dynasty may continue indefinitely.

GLOSSARY

ALL-PRO—A player who is voted to the Pro Bowl.

BACKFIELD—Players whose position is behind the line of scrimmage.

CORNERBACK—Either of two defensive halfbacks stationed a short distance behind the linebackers and relatively near the sidelines.

DEFENSIVE END—A defensive player who plays on the end of the line and often next to the defensive tackle.

DEFENSIVE TACKLE—A defensive player who plays on the line and between the guard and end.

ELIGIBLE—A player who is qualified to be voted into the Hall of Fame.

END ZONE—The area on either end of a football field where players score touchdowns.

EXTRA POINT—The additional one-point score added after a player makes a touchdown. Teams earn extra points if the placekicker kicks the ball through the uprights of the goalpost, or if an offensive player crosses the goal line with the football before being tackled.

FIELD GOAL—A three-point score awarded when a placekicker kicks the ball through the uprights of the goalpost.

FULLBACK—An offensive player who often lines up farthest behind the front line.

FUMBLE—When a player loses control of the football.

GUARD—An offensive lineman who plays between the tackles and center.

GROUND GAME—The running game.

HALFBACK—An offensive player whose position is behind the line of scrimmage.

HALFTIME—The time period between the second and third quarters of a football game.

INTERCEPTION—When a defensive player catches a pass from an offensive player.

KICK RETURNER—An offensive player who returns kickoffs.

LINEBACKER—A defensive player whose position is behind the line of scrimmage.

LINEMAN—An offensive or defensive player who plays on the line of scrimmage.

PASS—To throw the ball.

PASS RECEIVER—An offensive player who runs pass routes and catches passes.

PLACEKICKER—An offensive player who kicks extra points and field goals. The placekicker also kicks the ball from a tee to the opponent after his team has scored.

PLAYOFFS—The postseason games played amongst the division winners and wild card teams which determines the Super Bowl champion.

PRO BOWL—The postseason All-Star game which showcases the NFL's best players.

PUNT—To kick the ball to the opponent.

QUARTER—One of four 15-minute time periods that makes up a football game.

QUARTERBACK—The backfield player who usually calls the signals for the plays.

REGULAR SEASON—The games played after the preseason and before the playoffs.

ROOKIE—A first-year player.

RUNNING BACK—A backfield player who usually runs with the ball.

RUSH—To run with the football.

SACK—To tackle the quarterback behind the line of scrimmage.

SAFETY—A defensive back who plays behind the linemen and linebackers. Also, two points awarded for tackling an offensive player in his own end zone when he's carrying the ball.

SPECIAL TEAMS—Squads of football players that perform special tasks (for example, kickoff team and punt-return team).

SPONSOR—A person or company that finances a football team.

SUPER BOWL—The NFL Championship game played between the AFC champion and the NFC champion.

T FORMATION—An offensive formation in which the fullback lines up behind the center and quarterback with one halfback stationed on each side of the fullback.

TACKLE—An offensive or defensive lineman who plays between the ends and the guards.

TAILBACK—The offensive back farthest from the line of scrimmage.

TIGHT END—An offensive lineman who is stationed next to the tackles, and who usually blocks or catches passes.

TOUCHDOWN—When one team crosses the goal line of the other team's end zone. A touchdown is worth six points.

TURNOVER—To turn the ball over to an opponent either by a fumble, an interception, or on downs.

UNDERDOG—The team that is picked to lose the game.

WIDE RECEIVER—An offensive player who is stationed relatively close to the sidelines and who usually catches passes.

WILD CARD—A team that makes the playoffs without winning its division.

ZONE PASS DEFENSE—A pass defense method where defensive backs defend a certain area of the playing field rather than individual pass receivers.

INDEX